Tefillin

Making the Connection

Table of Contents

Approbation of HaGaon HaRav Nosson Zvi Finkel, *shlita,* Rosh HaYeshiva, Yeshivas Mir, Jerusalem:

הרב ישראל יעקב אהרמן שליט"א לומד זה עתה כמה שנים
בישיבתנו הק' והצליח בתלמודו עם יר"ש הקודמת לחכמתו
והנו בעל מדות תרומיות ועכשיו רחש לבו דבר טוב והוציא
לאור קונטרס בענין תפילין מודרכים שיזכה להמשיך לעלות
במעלות התורה בגופו ונפשו מוקירו ומכבדו

חדש הרחמים תשנ"ג

הכו"ח לכבוד התורה והעמלים בה

נתן צבי פינקל

Approbation of HaGaon HaRav Avigdor Nebenzahl, *shlita,* Rav of the Old City, Jerusalem:

בס"ד א' כ' וראו כל עמי הארץ וגו' תשנ"ג ירושלם עיה"ק תובב"א

גם אני מצטרף בתשבחות לקונטרס בהלכות תפלין ממאורתו לזכות
הרבים לקיים מצות תפלין בדקדוק, והמחבר שליט"א עמל לברר ההלכה
וידיו רב לו. יזכה לברכת ברוך אשר יקים ולשאר ברכות האמורות
במחזיקי התורה, לומדי' ומלמדי',

באהבת שיר הלוים

אביגדור נבנצל

Approbation of HaGaon HaRav Yitzchak Berkowitz, *shlita,* Mashgiach Ruchani, Yeshivas Aish Hatorah:

As the phenomenon of the adult beginner in Judaism becomes commonplace, there is a growing need for clear practical guides in all areas of Halacha.

Having read through this booklet, it seems obvious to me that this is one such work.

May HaShem bless the author with the ability to contribute to the education of our fellow Jews for years to come.

Yitzchak Berkovitz

before doing any mitzvah and think about why you are doing it. Think to yourself, "I am doing this because I love Hashem and I want to make Him happy." We should remember that He gives us life, lets us breathe, allows us to use our physical abilities. Shouldn't we try to make him happy by following His commandments? This will personalize the mitzvah, awakening the feelings of love and gratitude that bring us closer to Him. Also, since Hashem created all pleasure, if we can get close to Him, then we will eventually feel a lasting and internal pleasure and joy.

The second suggestion is to study the *halachos,* the details of the mitzvah, until you know them so thoroughly that you can do the mitzvah as it should be done, wholly and completely, with joy and enthusiasm.

The mitzvah of tefillin is very beloved to Hashem, and is one of the most meaningful symbols of our relationship with Him. It would be a shame to waste the opportunity and spend our lives putting on tefillin incorrectly. The purpose of this booklet is to offer an understanding and appreciation of tefillin, as well as to provide a familiarity with the *halachos* — the right ways — to put them on and take care of them.

Naturally, the best way to learn the *halachos* of tefillin is to study them directly from the most authoritative source in recent generations, the *Mishnah Berurah.* Until you can do that, this booklet can give you a quick way to learn the basics of how to perform the mitzvah of tefillin properly.

I hope you will enjoy using this booklet and that it will give you a greater feeling for this special mitzvah. May we come to perform all the mitzvos with enthusiasm and love, and together bring the *Mashiach* speedily in our days.

That Your Days Be Lengthened

Meir, a husband and the father of three children, from Long Island, New York, recounts his story for us:

"In the middle of August, 2001, my wife, Sheri, came down with meningitis. Thank G-d she recovered, but the whole experience was overwhelming. With Rosh Hashanah approaching, I realized that it had been quite a while since I had last checked my tefillin and because of what happened to my wife as well, I decided to get them checked.

"On Monday morning, September 10, Sheri dropped my tefillin off with R' Moshe Lieberman, the *sofer* who agreed to check my tefillin. Early that afternoon, R' Lieberman called me in my office to deliver the bad news about the state of my tefillin. He told me that he was not happy with the letter *yud* in one of the verses of the *Shema* and some other letters as well. He said that we could ask a young child if he recognized the letters in order to determine whether the tefillin were kosher. However, he explained, even if the child were able to recognize the letters, my tefillin would only be minimally acceptable. I told R' Lieberman that I would not be comfortable with tefillin that were only minimally acceptable, and he agreed to meet with me at my house later that evening.

"At about 11:30 that night, R' Lieberman arrived at my house. He showed me the *parshiyos* that were in my tefillin (and the problems with the *yud* and the other letters). It was clear to me that I should purchase new *parshiyos*. I asked R' Lieberman if I could write him a check for the amount due. He was reluctant to take the check before the tefillin were completed, but I finally convinced him to take it, as I wanted to be sure that this transaction would be completed before Rosh Hashanah."

The next morning, Tuesday, September 11, terrorists hijacked and crashed two airplanes into the two World Trade Center towers in New York City. The North Tower was struck at 8:45 a.m. The devastation of the terrorist attack was the worst in American history.

"At 9:05," Meir relates, "the subway train I was in passed through the Cortland Street/World Trade Center station without opening its doors. When I exited the subway two minutes later at the next station, I heard the news that my office building had been subject to a terrorist attack. My heart began to race. I realized that since I was up so late with the *sofer*, I did not wake up in time to catch the earlier train which I had intended to take. Had I caught that train, I would have already been in my office on the 59th floor at the time of the attack!

"I was stunned when I remembered that the problem with my tefillin that kept me up so late was the letter *yud* in the verse, *lema'an yirbu yemaichem* ("in order that your days be lengthened"). I rushed to call my wife as soon as I could reach a phone, and then R' Lieberman to thank him for finding the problems with my tefillin."

It was Meir's love and dedication to the mitzvah of tefillin that motivated him to quickly change his parshiyos so they would be perfect. Maybe it was the merit of this special mitzvah that protected him that day, in fulfillment of the verse, "in order that your days be lengthened."

To Save a Soul

Rabbi Aharon Kotler (1892-1962), zt"l, was one of the greatest Torah sages and Jewish leaders in his time. His son recalled the following story:

"At the outset of World War II, everyone who had the necessary papers attempted to cross the border from Poland to Russia. My father, Reb Aharon, successfully managed to cross the border with the rest of our family. Shortly after he arrived, he realized that in the commotion he had left his tefillin behind. He decided to go back for them.

"Despite the danger and the pleas from family and friends, my father was determined to get his tefillin. That night, he crossed the border, reached the *beis midrash* (study hall), and found his tefillin intact.

"By then it was morning, so my father decided to remain in Poland that day and wait until nightfall before trying to return to Russia. He headed to one of the border villages to find a place to stay, knocked at the door of one of the farmhouses, and was invited to stay the night.

"My father began to speak with his host, and he discovered the man was Jewish, but knew nothing about his heritage. By then, it was full daylight, and my father took out his tefillin to *daven*.

"The man watched my father intently as he *davened*. When he finished, my father asked, 'Have you already put on tefillin this morning?'

"'I've never put them on in my life,' the man confessed.

"My father was shocked. He gave the man a brief introduction to tefillin and explained that one who wears tefillin is rewarded in the World to Come.

"The man agreed to put on the tefillin, and my father helped him.

"My father stayed in the farmhouse the rest of the day. In the dark hours of the night, he successfully crossed the border back into Russia.

"Years later, my father had a dream. A Polish farmer appeared and asked, 'Do you remember me? You stayed in my house in Poland, after retrieving your tefillin.'

"He told my father that after he died, he was called before the Heavenly Court. 'The evidence against me was overwhelming, and I was sure that I was doomed. Just then, one defending angel came forward, and recounted how I had put on tefillin. For that one mitzvah alone, I was granted a share in the World to Come. Thank you, *rebbi*!'

"The next morning, my father remarked, 'At the time, I thought that I had gone back for my tefillin. Now I see that Hashem sent me back to help a fellow Jew merit a bit of *Olam Haba* (the World to Come)."

Reprinted with permission from *Visions of Greatness*, by Rabbi Yosef Weiss; C.I.S. Publishers.

Signs of Eminence

A Story Told by Rabbi Paysach J. Krohn, *shlita**

The Gemara (Shabbos 130a) recounts a remarkable incident involving a pious man named Elisha.

It seems that Elisha, unlike others who were afraid, defied the Roman authorities who decreed that any Jew caught wearing tefillin on his head would be killed. Elisha boldly disregarded this threat and bravely wore his tefillin in public.

One day a Roman officer spotted Elisha wearing his tefillin. Realizing that he had been seen, Elisha began to run away, but the officer gave chase and caught up with him. Elisha snatched the tefillin off his head and covered them with both hands.

"What is in your hands?" demanded the officer.

"I am carrying wings of a dove," said Elisha.

The Gemara relates that miraculously, when Elisha opened his hands, he indeed was carrying the wings of a dove.

From then on he was referred to as Elisha *Baal Kenafayim* (Elisha, man of wings), an eternal tribute to his commitment to this sacred mitzvah.**

In our era, too, there lived a pious Jew with an extraordinary commitment to the hallowed mitzvah of tefillin. In life's most dire circumstances, he risked his life so that he and others like him could observe this daily mitzvah.

His story was retold by family members who rightfully regard their relative with awe, as should we.

In 1940, R' Binyamin Schachner was hauled from his home in the small

---

* Reprinted with permission from *In the Footsteps of the Maggid*,
  by Rabbi Paysach J. Krohn; Artscroll/Mesorah Publications.
** Indeed, some people are accustomed to wrap the *retzuos* (straps) of their *tefillin shel rosh*
  over both sides of the tefillin (on the *titurah*, the base on which the tefillin rests) to
  resemble the wings of a dove (*Mishnah Berurah, Orach Chaim* 28, note 9).

town of Susnofsza, Poland to the first of seven concentration camps he was eventually to be in. Among the few possessions that he managed to take along with him were his tefillin. R' Binyamin always kept a close watch on his tefillin, shielding and safeguarding them as though they were his life's greatest treasure. Every day, when he was sure that none of the Nazi guards were looking, he would remove the tefillin from their hiding place, don them on his hand and head, and say the *Shema*.

Others in his barracks, inspired by his actions, would borrow the tefillin and do the same.

R' Binyamin was transferred from concentration camp to concentration camp until he was eventually brought to a slave labor camp in Markstadt.

Aside from the toil demanded and torture inflicted there daily, this place was an area of such filth and of conditions so inhuman that survival was difficult. Food was scarce and hard to come by, and every day Jews perished from disease and starvation.

When he first came to Markstadt, R' Binyamin was confronted by an SS guard who demanded to know whether he was a carpenter. Instinctively, he replied that he was, although actually he had never built anything in his life except a family. Because he knew that those deemed "useless" were put to death at once, R' Binyamin decided to claim that he was, indeed, handy. In order to survive he would try anything.

It was in the carpenters' woodshed, under a loose floorboard, that R' Binyamin hid his tefillin while he was in Markstadt. Throughout the weeks and months of his stay, every day without fail, he and others who dared, would disregard their privation and exhaustion and remove the tefillin from under the loose wooden plank. Each man would, in turn, wrap the tefillin around his hand and on his head and tearfully say the *Shema*, proclaiming, even in his most dire of situations, the uniqueness and Oneness of Hashem and *Klal Yisrael*'s devoted loyalty to Him. Then the tefillin would be hidden away once again.

One day a particularly vicious SS guard walked into the woodshed unexpectedly and saw the tefillin. Realizing that this must be a religious item of sorts, he began to scream in bloodcurdling tones, demanding to know what and whose they were. Frozen with terror, no one dared say a word.

The Nazi began to yell again, this time threatening to kill everyone in the room if he didn't get a reply.

R' Binyamin's words somehow made it out of his throat. "This used to belong to a young boy who died recently," he said softly.

"But if he died, and you all kept these things here, then they belong to you now," the guard retorted in anger. And with that he ordered R' Binyamin to come outside with him.

R' Binyamin had no choice but to obey, for if he didn't comply now he would be killed immediately. Outside, and within the hearing of those inside the shed, the guard began to beat R' Binyamin mercilessly. His screams and cries pierced the hearts of everyone inside until they could stand it no longer. They ran to the barracks' kapo (Nazi-appointed leader — who in this case was a Jewish informer) and beseeched him to go out to the Nazi guard and beg for mercy. None of the regular inmates would dare ask the Nazi soldier for a favor; only someone who had the confidence of the oppressors could even make an attempt.

R' Binyamin's friends knew that only the kapo could intervene on his behalf. The kapo pleaded with the Nazi guard, who finally agreed to stop beating R' Binyamin. The Nazi then ordered R' Binyamin to march back into the barracks. When he walked in, the others were shocked by his appearance. He was bleeding from multiple body wounds and was clutching his ear. (His hearing was impaired for the rest of his life from that beating.)

The guard ordered that the religious articles be burned at once, and he announced that he would be coming back to see that it was in flames.

R' Binyamin didn't say a word to anyone but went right over to the shelf where he had his tools and scraps of wood. He brought them to his workbench and, as fast as he could, he began to carve little square boxes to resemble tefillin. He glued the sides together as the others around him watched, astonished by his courage and ingenious idea.

A few men built a fire, and soon the boxes were tossed in. Two people removed their leather belts and threw them into the fire as well, to resemble the *retzuos* (straps) of the tefillin that had once again been hidden.

The guard came in, saw the fire, inspected it closely and walked out with a satisfied smile on his devious face. But the tefillin now securely hidden, remained intact. R' Binyamin and his friends cried as they thanked Hashem for this miracle amidst their agony.

R' Binyamin guarded and protected his tefillin for the remaining time of his incarceration at Markstadt. When he was finally liberated, his treasured tefillin were still intact, and he was able to leave the camp clutching them tightly in his hands.

* * *

Now, decades later, the precious legacy of R' Binyamin's adherence to the mitzvah of tefillin lives on. The tefillin were recently checked by a *sofer* (scribe) who verified that they are perfectly valid. However, he did advise against their being used on a regular basis. Today every grandson of R' Binyamin is given the honor of putting on these extraordinary tefillin on the day of his bar mitzvah.

Tefillin have always symbolized the boy who becomes a man.
Tefillin in this case symbolize how a man became a legend.

HOW TO PUT ON TEFILLIN
An Illustrated Guide

PREPARATIONS

- Make sure you don't have to go to the bathroom.[1]
- Clean off anything that is stuck to your arm or head in the place where the *batim* (the black casings) in which the four *parshiyos* (Torah portions) rest.[2]
- It is advisable to remove your watch.
- The *retzuah* (black leather strap) may be wound over a cast or a bandage.[3]
- Your arm and head should be completely dry before putting on the tefillin. Wetness can warp the tefillin and render them non-kosher.
- If you wear a *tallis*, put the *tallis* on first, before the tefillin.[4]
- Place the tefillin bag on a secure, flat surface so they will not fall.
- The bag should be resting with the top side up and the opening facing you.
- The *tefillin shel yad* (the tefillin worn on the arm) is put on before the *tefillin shel rosh* (the tefillin worn on the head).

THE PROCEDURE FOR PUTTING ON THE *TEFILLIN SHEL YAD*

1) Put your right hand (a lefty uses his left hand) into the left side of the bag and remove the *tefillin shel yad*.[5]

Do not touch the *tefillin shel rosh* first.[6]

Remove the tefillin with respect.

2) Remove and uncoil the *retzuah* from the box.

Be careful never to let the *retzuah* touch the floor.[7]

3) Loosen the *retzuah* beneath the box, invert the box slightly, and carefully remove the *bayis* (the black casing).

Check to see that the *yud kesher* (the knot on the tefillin) has not separated from the *bayis*. If it did, then move it back to the *bayis*.[8]

Those who follow Minhag Chabad will move and check the *yud kesher* at a later stage.

4) It is respectful to kiss the tefillin before putting them on.[9]

5) Roll up your left sleeve (a lefty rolls up his right sleeve) above your bicep.

6) Before putting on the tefillin you must have the proper *kavanah* (intent), keeping in mind the purpose of the mitzvah. Verbalize or think to yourself, "I am putting on tefillin because G-d commanded me to wear tefillin containing the four *parshiyos*, 'Kadesh li chol bechor,' 'Vehayah ki yeviacha,' 'Shema,' 'Vehayah im shamoa,' that discuss the Oneness of Hashem and the Exodus from Egypt. I am putting tefillin on my arm near my heart and on my head, to demonstrate that I dedicate my strength, my heart, and my mind to the service of G-d." Some people say the paragraph in the *siddur* to help them have the right *kavanah* for the mitzvah.[10]

Ashkenazim put on the *tefillin shel yad* while standing; Sephardim put on the *shel yad* while sitting.[11]

7) Be sure that the *ma'abarta* (the portion of the base through which the strap passes) does not extend past the midpoint line of the bicep (a).[12]

Place the *bayis* on the lower part of the bicep, and tilt it towards the body.[13]

Be sure that the front of the *titurah* (the square base on which the *bayis* rests) does not extend past the lowest end of the bicep (b).[14]

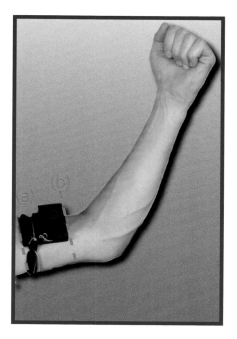

You can check for the lowest end by flexing your muscle, or by placing two fingers between your forearm and your bicep (assuming that this area has the exact space of two fingers).

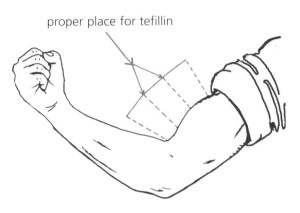

proper place for tefillin

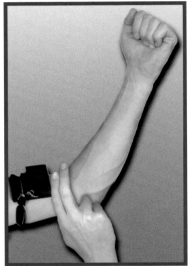

One who has large tefillin should place them a little higher up, rather than going beyond the muscle.

If the tefillin rest at all below the muscle, the mitzvah has not been fulfilled.[15]

Check that your sleeve isn't caught under the *bayis* or in the *retzuah*.[16]

Minhag Sefard* and Minhag of Sephardim   **Minhag Ashkenaz**

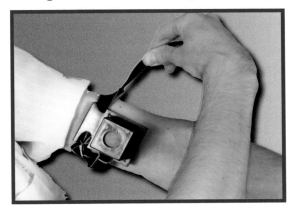
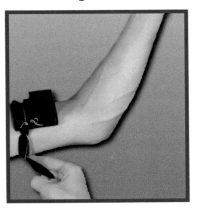

8) While holding the *retzuah* near the *bayis* with your right hand before tightening it, recite the following *berachah*:

בָּרוּךְ אַתָּה יי אֱלֹהֵינוּ מֶלֶךְ הָעוֹלָם,
אֲשֶׁר קִדְּשָׁנוּ בְּמִצְוֹתָיו וְצִוָּנוּ לְהָנִיחַ תְּפִלִּין:

"Baruch Attah, Ado-nai, Elo-heinu, Melech HaOlam,
asher kideshanu bemitzvosav, vetzivanu lehawniach tefillin." [17]

It is important to pronounce the *kamatz* in לְהָנִיחַ as *lehawniach*, and not *lehaniach*, so as not to suggest another meaning of the word.[18]

Have in mind that this berachah also applies for the *tefillin shel rosh*.

Check that the *"yud"* knot is always pressed against the *bayis*.

Be careful that there be no interruption between putting on the *tefillin shel yad* and the *tefillin shel rosh*. Please see page 49 for details.

HELPFUL HINT: Those who follow Minhag Ashkenaz can use the underside of their forearm to hold the tefillin in the proper place while making the *berachah* until the tefillin are fastened to the bicep.

HELPFUL HINT: Those who follow Minhag Sefard and Sepharadim, may find it helpful to keep the tefillin in place until the *retzuah* is fastened, by pressing the top of the bayis into the side of one's body.

*Minhag Sefard is a custom of many Ashkenazic Jews.

9) Immediately following the *berachah,* tighten the *retzuah* and wind the *retzuah* around the forearm.[19]

Minhag Sefard and Minhag of Sephardim

Pull the *retzuah* away from the body, under the upper arm and towards the fore-arm, and then wrap it around the forearm eight times (seven complete times). The remain-

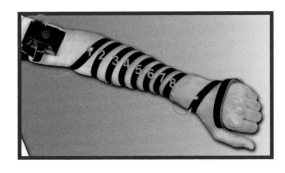

der of the *retzuah* should be wound around your palm.

Minhag Ashkenaz

Pull the *retzuah* under and then over the upper arm towards the forearm and then wrap it seven times around the forearm. The remainder of the *retzuah* should be wound around your palm.

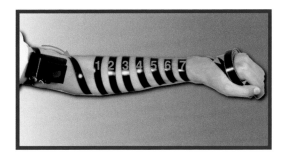

10) Check that the *titurah* doesn't pass the lower end of the bicep. Check that the *bayis* is sufficiently slanted towards your body. Lower your arm against the side of your body to see that the *bayis* touches your body.

If at any time while wearing tefillin, the *bayis* slips below the muscle, it must be moved back into place. If the *retzuah* slips down your arm, tighten the slack.

(continue on page 31)

Minhag Chabad

8) While holding the *retzuah* near the loop with your right hand before tightening it, recite the following *berachah*:

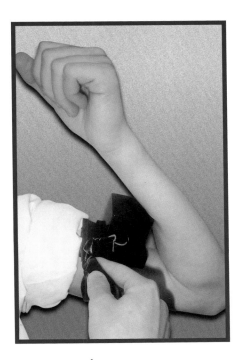

בָּרוּךְ אַתָּה יי
אֱלֹהֵינוּ מֶלֶךְ הָעוֹלָם,
אֲשֶׁר קִדְּשָׁנוּ בְּמִצְוֹתָיו
וְצִוָּנוּ לְהָנִיחַ תְּפִלִּין:

"Baruch Attah, Ado-nai, Elo-heinu, Melech HaOlam, asher kideshanu bemitzvosav, vetzivanu lehawniach tefillin." [17]

It is important to pronounce the *kamatz* in לְהָנִיחַ as *lehawniach*, and not *lehaniach*, so as not to suggest another meaning of the word. [18]

Have in mind that this *berachah* also applies for the *tefillin shel rosh*.

Be careful that there be no unnecessary pausing, gesturing or talking between putting on the *tefillin shel yad* and the *tefillin shel rosh*.

9) Immediately following the *berachah*, tighten the *retzuah* by pulling the *retzuah* completely through the loop until the loop is completely closed. One helpful method may be to use your right thumb and forefinger to pull the *retzuah* through the loop while pressing your left forearm against the *bayis* to keep it in place. Check that the *"yud"* knot is pressed against the *bayis*.

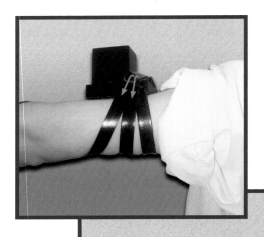

Minhag Chabad continued:
Tightly wrap the *retzuah* two times around the *ma'abarta* so that the letter "*shin*" is formed with the *retzuah* that is resting on the outside of your arm.

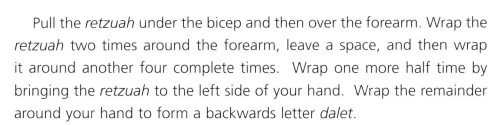

Pull the *retzuah* under the bicep and then over the forearm. Wrap the *retzuah* two times around the forearm, leave a space, and then wrap it around another four complete times. Wrap one more half time by bringing the *retzuah* to the left side of your hand. Wrap the remainder around your hand to form a backwards letter *dalet*.

10) Check that the *titurah* doesn't pass the lower end of the bicep. Check that the *bayis* is sufficiently slanted towards your body. Lower your arm against the side of your body to see that the *bayis* touches your body.

If at any time while wearing tefillin, the *bayis* slips below the muscle, it must be moved back into place. If the *retzuah* slips down your arm, tighten the slack.

THE PROCEDURE FOR PUTTING ON THE *TEFILLIN SHEL ROSH*

1) Immediately after putting on and checking the placement of the *tefillin shel yad*, place your right hand into the tefillin bag (a lefty uses his left hand) and respectfully take out the *tefillin shel rosh*.

2) Remove and uncoil the *retzuah* from the box. Be careful not to let the *retzuah* touch the floor.

3) Loosen the *retzuah* beneath the box, invert the box slightly, and carefully remove the *bayis*.

4) It is respectful to kiss the tefillin before putting them on.

5) Ashkenazim and Sephardim stand to put on the *tefillin shel rosh*.[20]

6) Place the *tefillin shel rosh* on your head in its proper place and place the *retzuah* loosely around your head. Sephardim and those who follow Minhag Chabad should fasten the *retzuah* onto the head by pushing the *retzuah* down with one's fingertips. The proper place for the *tefillin shel rosh* is as follows:

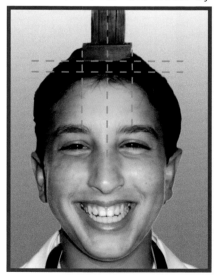

a) The *titurah* must not be lower than the hairline (or where the hairline used to be). Therefore it is advisable to place the *bayis* slightly above the hairline, in case it slips down a bit.

b) The tefillin should be lined up exactly between your eyes (directly above your nose).

c) The *kesher* (the knot on the *retzuah)* should be centered on the bump at the base of your skull. Press your finger on the center of the knot. If you feel pressure against the bump, the knot has been properly centered.[21]

Check that:

■ The *retzuah* is not twisted and the black side faces outward.

■ Your *yarmulke* is not under the *bayis* or the *retzuah.*

Please note that the mitzvah has not been fulfilled:

■ If the tefillin rest at all below the original hairline.

■ If the knot on the back of your head rests on your neck.

You may also look in a mirror to check your tefillin.

7) Before tightening the *retzuah,* keep your fingers on the *retzuah* on both sides of your head and recite the following *berachah:*

בָּרוּךְ אַתָּה יי אֱלֹהֵינוּ מֶלֶךְ הָעוֹלָם,
אֲשֶׁר קִדְּשָׁנוּ בְּמִצְוֹתָיו וְצִוָּנוּ עַל-מִצְוַת תְּפִלִּין:

"Baruch Attah, Ado-nai, Elo-heinu, Melech HaOlam, asher kideshanu bemitzvosav, vetzivanu al mitzvas tefillin." [22]

Sephardim and those who follow Minhag Chabad do not recite a *berachah* on the *tefillin shel rosh.*[23]

Note that the second-to-last word in this *berachah* is *"mitzvas"* and not *"mitzvos."* [24]

8) Immediately fasten the *retzuah* onto your head by pushing it down with your fingertips.[25]

Check that the *bayis* and the *kesher* are in the proper place with the following suggested methods:

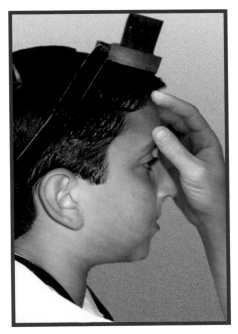

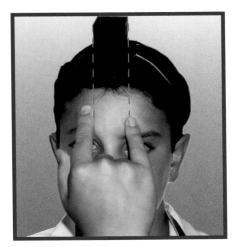

b) Check that the *bayis* is centered by grasping the sides of its base with your second and fifth fingers and sliding them down over your nose. If your nose is not lined up between your two bent fingers, then re-center your tefillin.

a) Touch the hairline to make sure that the end of the *titurah* does not pass your original hairline.

c) Check that the knot is centered and is also not on your neck.

When everything is secured in its proper place, Ashkenazim silently say:

בָּרוּךְ שֵׁם כְּבוֹד מַלְכוּתוֹ לְעוֹלָם וָעֶד:

"Baruch sheim kevod malchuso le'olam va'ed." [26]

At this point, some have the custom to say the paragraph beginning with the word *u'mechochmasah*, which can be found in the *siddur*.

9) Check that the *retzuah* hangs down on both sides of your head, over your shoulders, and that the black side is showing.[27]

If the *bayis* of the *tefillin shel rosh* does not stay above the hairline, the knot must be adjusted. Please see page 65 for instructions.

THE PROCEDURE FOR WRAPPING THE *RETZUAH* AROUND THE HAND

Minhag Ashkenaz

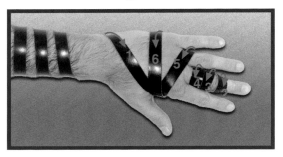

(There are different *minhagim* regarding how to wrap the *retzuah* around the hand.)

a) After checking the *tefillin shel rosh*, unwind the *retzuah* from your hand.

b) Bring the *retzuah* to the middle finger and wrap it once between the second and third knuckles (2).

c) Wrap it around the same finger two more times, between your second knuckle and the hand knuckle (3 & 4).

d) Form a *shin* by first making a "V" (5 & 6) and then wrapping the *retzuah* a few times on the middle part of the *shin* (6). You can tuck in the remainder around the middle of the *shin*.

(Minhag Ashkenaz, continued on page 38)

Minhag Sefard

(There are different *minhagim* regarding how to wrap the *retzuah* around the hand.)

a) After checking the *tefillin shel rosh*, unwind the *retzuah* from your hand.

b) Bring the *retzuah* to the middle finger and wrap it once between the second and third knuckles (2).

c) Wrap it around the same finger two more times, between your second knuckle and the hand knuckle (3 & 4).

d) Wrap it around the middle and fourth fingers to complete the letter *dalet* (5).

e) Form a *shin* by first making a "V" (6 & 7) and then wrapping the *retzuah* a few times on the middle part of the *shin* (7). You can tuck in the remainder around the middle of the *shin*.

(Minhag Sefard, continued on page 38)

Minhag of Sephardim

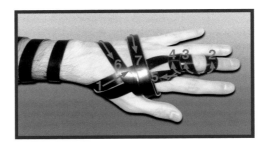

(There are different *minhagim* regarding how to wrap the *retzuah* around the hand.)

a) After checking the *tefillin shel rosh*, completely unwind the *retzuah* from your hand.

b) Bring the *retzuah* from the right side of your wrist over your hand, through the space between your third and fourth fingers (1).

c) Wrap the *retzuah* around the middle finger, between the second and third knuckles (2).

d) Wrap it around the same finger two more times, between the second knuckle and the hand knuckle (3)&(4).

e) Bring the *retzuah* between the space between the second and third fingers and back over your hand (5).

f) Pull the *retzuah* under your wrist and bring it back across your hand on a slant (6).

g) Wrap the remainder of the *retzuah* over the middle of your hand (7). Tuck in the end.

(Minhag of Sephardim, continued on page 38)

Minhag Chabad

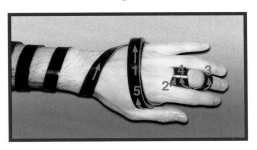

a) After checking the *tefillin shel rosh*, unwind the *retzuah* from your hand except for the last wrapping (the original letter *dalet)* (1).

b) Bring the *retzuah* under your hand to the middle finger and wrap it once between the hand knuckle and the second knuckle (2).

c) Wrap it around the same finger, between the second and third knuckles (3).

d) Wrap it a third time around the same finger, between the hand knuckle and the second knuckle (4).

e) The remainder of the *retzuah* should be wrapped around the hand and tucked in securely at the end (5).

■ Some people have a custom to say this verse while wrapping the *retzuah* three times around the middle finger:

וְאֵרַשְׂתִּיךְ לִי לְעוֹלָם,

"Ve'airastich li le'olam" (initial wrap around middle finger);

וְאֵרַשְׂתִּיךְ לִי בְּצֶדֶק וּבְמִשְׁפָּט וּבְחֶסֶד וּבְרַחֲמִים:

"Ve'airastich li be'tzedek u'vemishpat u'vechesed u'verachamim"

(second wrap around middle finger);

וְאֵרַשְׂתִּיךְ לִי בֶּאֱמוּנָה וְיָדַעַתְּ אֶת־יי:

"Ve'airastich li be'emunah, veyada'at es Ado-nai"

(third wrap around middle finger).

Some say the *parshiyos* of *"Kadesh li chol bechor"* and *"Vehayah ki yeviacha"* after putting on tefillin. They can be found in your *siddur.*

■ Cover the *tefillin shel yad* with your shirt or jacket sleeve.

HOW TO REMOVE YOUR TEFILLIN

Ashkenazim and Sephardim stand for the removal of the *tefillin shel rosh.*[28]

Take off your *tallis* after removing your tefillin.[29]

■ Unwind the *retzuah* from the hand and wrap the removed part around your palm.

■ Remove the *tefillin shel rosh* with the left hand[30] (a lefty removes it with the right hand), kiss the *bayis,* and put it into the box for the *tefillin shel rosh.*[31]

- Some people have a custom to wrap the *retzuah* on both sides of the box to resemble the wings of doves.[32]

- Place the *kesher* on top of the base of the box and not under it (since the *kesher* forms the letter *dalet*, which is one of the letters of G-d's name).[33]

- Hold the box stationary and wrap the *retzuah* around it.[34]

- Place the *tefillin shel rosh* into the right side of the tefillin bag.[35]

- Ashkenazim stand to remove the *tefillin shel yad*. Sephardim sit.[36]

- Unwind the *retzuah* of the *tefillin shel yad*, take off the *bayis,* kiss it, and put it into the box.

- Some have a *minhag* to wrap the *retzuah* on both sides of the box; others wrap it on the side which doesn't have the *yud kesher*.[37]

- One should be careful not to let the *retzuah* touch the floor.

- The *tefillin shel yad* should be placed into the left side of the tefillin bag, slightly closer to the opening of the bag than the *tefillin shel rosh*.[38]

OTHER *HALACHOS* AND *MINHAGIM* OF CHABAD

If after reciting the *berachah* "*Lehawniach*," and before tightening the *retzuah*, you talked about something that is not necessary to completing the mitzvah of tefillin, loosen the *tefillin shel yad*, repeat the *berachah* on it, and tighten it. If you talked after tightening the *tefillin shel yad*, finish wrapping the *retzuah* around your arm, and recite the *berachah* "*al mitzvas tefillin*" on the *tefillin shel rosh*. Follow the procedures for putting on the *tefillin shel rosh* (according to non-Chabad *minhagim*) on the pages to follow. Minhag Chabad, however, is not to say the words "*Baruch sheim kevod…*"

However, if after fastening the *tefillin shel yad* to your arm, you hear the congregation saying the following, you should answer with them:

In *Kaddish*: *"Amein. Y'hei sh'mei rabbah…yis'barach."*

In *Barechu*: *"Baruch Hashem hamevorach leolam vaed."*

In *Kedushah*: *"Kadosh…," "Baruch…," "Yimloch…."*

In *Modim*: Only the words *"Modim anachnu lach."*

In *Bircas HaTorah*: *"Baruch Hashem hamevorach leolam vaed,"* and *"Amein"* after *"Nosein HaTorah."*

Other *berachos*: *"Amein"* after *"Hakel Hakadosh,"* and *"Shomeiya Tefillah."*

After hearing thunder: *"Baruch…shekocho ugevuroso malei olam."*

After seeing lightening: *"Baruch…oseh ma'asei vereishis."*

Please note that you may answer with the congregation even before you wind the *retzuah* around the forearm as long as the *bayis* will not slip out of place.

If you did answer with the congregation, be sure to recite the *berachah "al mitzvas tefillin"* on the *tefillin shel rosh*. Follow the procedures for putting on the *tefillin shel rosh* (according to non-Chabad *minhagim*) on the pages to follow. Do not, however, say the words *"Baruch sheim kevod…"* The *minhag* of Chabad is not to say *"ve'airastich li"* while wrapping the *retzuah* around the finger.

The *minhag* of Chabad is to start putting on tefillin two months before one's thirteenth Jewish birth date. One may start to recite a *berachah* after a few weeks of learning how to put on tefillin properly.

Minhag Chabad is to also put on an additional pair of tefillin that contain *parshiyos* that are placed inside the *bayis* according to the order of the Rabbeinu Tam, Rashi's grandson. The placement of *Vehayah im shamoa* precedes *Shema*. The *minhag* today is to start putting on Rabbeinu Tam tefillin at the same age when one starts to put on Rashi tefillin.

Rabbeinu Tam tefillin should ideally be put on immediately after the conclusion of the prayer service. If it is impossible to do this, you may put them on any time throughout the day. When reciting a *berachah* on the Rashi tefillin, it is proper to have in mind the Rabbeinu Tam tefillin as well. Although a *berachah* is not recited upon the Rabbeinu Tam tefillin, one should not interrupt the placement of the *tefillin shel yad* and the *tefillin shel rosh*. One may answer with the congregation for those prayers as permitted for the Rashi tefillin.

While wearing the Rabbeinu Tam tefillin, read the three *parshiyos* of *Shema Yisrael*, and the *parshiyos* of *Vehayah ki yeviacha*, and *Kadesh li*. In addition, it is the custom to say the *Six Remembrances*.

On *Rosh Chodesh*, remove the Rashi tefillin after the *Sefer Torah* has been put back into the ark, and put on the Rabbeinu Tam tefillin. Say the *parshiyos* of *Shema Yisrael*, *Kadesh li*, and *Vehayah ki yeviacha*, and remove the tefillin before the Half *Kaddish* that precedes *Mussaf*.

One should have two separate bags for the Rashi tefillin and the Rabbeinu Tam tefillin. One should have a sign on each bag to recognize which tefillin are inside.

QUESTIONS AND ANSWERS
Halachos of Tefillin

BUYING TEFILLIN

Should I spend a lot of money to buy tefillin?

Everyone should buy tefillin that are **unquestionably** kosher even though they may be expensive. If you have the means, it is praiseworthy to spend extra money on a higher standard of craftsmanship and beauty. If you find tefillin that are being sold at a very cheap price, usually there are things wrong with them.[39]

From whom should I buy my tefillin?

You should buy tefillin only from an expert *sofer* (scribe) or from a store owner who is a G-d-fearing person and is trusted by the community.[40] It is advisable to ask a rabbi to recommend a trustworthy *sofer*.

Please feel free to contact this author if you need assistance.

Tefillin is the strength of the Jewish People. It is written (Deuteronomy 28:10), "And the peoples of the earth will see that G-d's name is called upon you, and they shall be awed by you."

Berachos 6a

WHEN TO PUT ON TEFILLIN

When are tefillin worn?

Tefillin are put on before beginning *Shacharis* and worn every day except Shabbos, Rosh Hashanah, Yom Kippur, Succos, Pesach, and Shavuos. There are different *minhagim* regarding wearing tefillin on *Chol Hamoed,* and you should act according to your *minhag.*[41]

At what age does one start putting on tefillin?

Although the Biblical obligation starts from the day a boy reaches his thirteenth birthday (according to the Jewish calendar), it is customary to start putting on tefillin (with a *berachah*) a month before one becomes bar mitzvah, in order to become accustomed to the mitzvah. One may begin putting them on at this age only if he can control his bodily functions.[42]

When should I wear tefillin on Tishah b'Av?

On Tishah b'Av tefillin are not worn during *Shacharis*; however, they are put on for *Minchah*. Do not recite *Kerias Shema* during *Minchah*, because it is considered like reading from the Torah, an act prohibited on Tishah b'Av.[43]

What is the earliest time in the day I can put on tefillin?

The *zeman tefillin* (the earliest time that tefillin may be put on in the morning) is when there is enough natural light out to recognize a somewhat familiar person from a distance of six to eight feet.[44] This is usually slightly less than an hour before sunrise. One who *must* put on tefillin earlier than this time should consult a rabbi.[45]

What is the latest time in the day I can put on tefillin?

You may put them on with a *berachah* until *shkiyas hachamah* (sunset), and without a *berachah* until nightfall.[46]

Rabbi Chiya bar Abba said in the name of Rabbi Yochanan, "A man who washes his hands, puts on tefillin, says the Shema and prays, is considered to have built an altar and offered a sacrifice."

Berachos 15a

If I have a severely upset stomach at the time of *davening*, should I still put on tefillin?

You must be able to control your bodily functions while wearing tefillin. If you are **certain beyond a doubt** that you will not be able to *daven* without constantly passing gas or running to the bathroom, it is better to wait and *daven* later. However, be sure to recite the *Shema* (without tefillin) before its time limit.[47]

If it is physically possible later, and you haven't *davened* yet, but the latest time for saying the *Shemoneh Esrei* of *Shacharis* has passed,

a) put on tefillin and say *Shema* or a paragraph of *Tehillim,* and

b) *daven Shemoneh Esrei* twice during *Minchah.*

If, during the regular *davening* time, it is possible to put on tefillin only for a few minutes, put them on with a *berachah* after *Ahavah Rabbah* (the *berachah* preceding *Shema*) and remove them after *Kerias Shema*.[48]

If I have aches and pains in other parts of my body, should I put on tefillin?

If you have other illnesses, you are exempt from tefillin only if the pain is too great for you to concentrate on wearing tefillin. Later in the day, if you feel better, put on tefillin immediately.[49]

Wearing tefillin is like reading from the Torah.
Pesikta Zutrasa, Shemos 13

PUTTING ON TEFILLIN

Should I make the *berachah* "*Shehechiyanu*" when I wear tefillin for the first time?

If you normally make a "*Shehechiyanu*" on a new garment, put on the new garment for the first time and put on your tefillin. First recite the *berachos* on the tefillin, followed by the *berachah* "*Shehechiyanu.*" [50]

Do I fulfill the mitzvah of tefillin if I don't think about why I'm putting them on?

You are required to have the purpose of the mitzvah of tefillin in mind at some point either just before putting them on or while you're wearing them. Please see step #6 on page 25 for details. It is a particularly important time to concentrate on what you are doing. If you didn't have the proper intent in mind, yet removed your tefillin, you have fulfilled the mitzvah of tefillin, but not in its fullest form.[51]

> **When a man wakes up in the morning and binds himself with the holy mark of tefillin, four angels greet him as he goes out the door.**
>
> **Zohar Chadash, Terumah**

May I smile or nod at someone while I am putting on tefillin?

You are forbidden to do anything at all, including talking, gesturing, smiling, winking, or even pausing unnecessarily, from the time you tighten the strap of the *tefillin shel yad* on your arm until after the *tefillin shel rosh* is securely positioned on your head.[52]

If the congregation is saying *Shema*, *Kaddish*, or *Kedushah* during this time, you should not answer with them but rather listen to what they are saying and think the appropriate responses in your mind. The one exception to this is if you find yourself in a situation where you cannot complete the mitzvah of tefillin without talking (e.g. to ask a rabbi or some other knowledgeable person how to proceed).

If you did talk during this time, even accidentally, you should loosen the *tefillin shel yad*, repeat the *berachah* on it, and tighten it; then put on the *tefillin shel rosh* as usual. The first *berachah* is considered to have been said in vain even if all you did was respond *amen* or *borchu* and the like. This last halachah applies only to speech and not to any of the other interruptions.[53]

The Messiah will come to give the world mitzvos such as tefillin.

Midrash Tehillim 21

If my tefillin slip out of place during *davening,* do I recite another *berachah* to put them back in the proper place?

If in the middle of *davening* your tefillin slip out of place, or you take them off for the purpose of fixing them, you do not have to recite another *berachah* when putting them back on.[54]

What happens if I put on tefillin incorrectly (e.g. on the wrong place), or if I put on non-kosher tefillin?

If tefillin are worn on the wrong place on the arm or head, **it is as if they never left the bag and no mitzvah is fulfilled.**[55] Similarly, one cannot fulfill the mitzvah with non-kosher tefillin, and any *berachos* one makes are considered to have been made in vain.[56]

When a man wears tefillin,
a voice proclaims to all the angels
of the Chariot who watch over prayer,
"Give honor to the image of the King,
the man who wears tefillin."
Tikunei Zohar 124a

Are there certain times during *davening* when I should touch my tefillin to remind myself that I am wearing them?

During the *Shema*, when you say "*Ukeshartem le'os al yadecha*" you should touch the *tefillin shel yad*; and when you say "*vehayu letotafos bein einecha*" you should touch the *tefillin shel rosh*. (In this and all the instances mentioned below, it is customary to kiss your fingers after each time you touch either the *tefillin shel yad* or the *tefillin shel rosh*.) Similarly, in "*Ukeshartem le'os al yedchem*" and "*vehayu letotafos bein einechem*" in the second paragraph of the *Shema*.[57] In *Ashrei*, some touch the *tefillin shel yad* at "*Posei'ach es yadecha*," and the *tefillin shel rosh* at "*u'masbia lechol chai ratzon*"; and at "*yotzair ohr*" (*tefillin shel yad*) and "*u'voreih choshech*" (*shel rosh*) in the first *berachah* before the *Shema*.[58]

G-d loved the Jewish people so much
that He surrounded them with mitzvos;
tefillin on the head and arm,
tzitzis on their garments,
and a mezuzah on their doors.

Menachos 43b

PROPER DECORUM WHILE WEARING TEFILLIN

How should I be dressed while wearing tefillin?

When you get dressed for *davening* keep in mind that you are about to stand in front of the King.

You may not put on tefillin without wearing a shirt.[59]

What should I do if I have to pass gas or use the bathroom while wearing tefillin?

Always go to the bathroom before putting on tefillin, as it is strictly forbidden to pass gas while wearing tefillin. If you feel you won't be able to hold back from passing gas, you should move your tefillin out of their proper place. Move the *shel rosh* to the side and loosen the *retzuah*, and move the *shel yad* below your bicep and loosen the *retzuah*. Then, afterwards, put the tefillin back in their appropriate places, recite the *berachos* on the tefillin again, and tighten the *retzuos*.

Remove your tefillin before using the bathroom. After defecating, put the tefillin on again and recite the *berachos* on them.[60] There are different factors regarding the recitation of *berachos* on tefillin after urinating. One should consult a Rabbi.

Is there anything I should not be thinking about while wearing tefillin?

You should not have any lustful thoughts while wearing tefillin and otherwise.[61] If you are having trouble controlling these thoughts, try learning more Torah and *Mussar* (Jewish texts that discuss self-growth and improvement, e.g. *The Path of the Just*),[62] or get advice from someone you trust.

May I tell a joke while wearing tefillin?

You should always remember your tefillin when you are wearing them. Therefore you should not joke around or say things that will lead to laughter and lightheadedness.[63]

May I eat while wearing my tefillin?

It is prohibited to eat a meal of bread while wearing tefillin. However, you may eat the equivalent of the size of an egg of: bread, cake or cookies. There is no restriction for eating fruits and non-intoxicating beverages. You should not drink an amount of wine or alcohol that will make you drunk.[64]

May I doze off while wearing tefillin?

You may not fall into a regular sleep while wearing tefillin. If you start dozing off while wearing tefillin, it is advisable to remove them.[65]

May I wear tefillin near garbage that has a bad smell?

If the smell irritates you to the point where you become disgusted, it is prohibited.[66]

He who wears tefillin is worthy of long life.
Menachos 44a

REMOVING TEFILLIN

When should I remove my tefillin?

If possible, you should leave your tefillin on until after the mourner's *Kaddish* which follows *Aleinu*.[67] If for some reason you have to leave shul early, you should take care not to do any of the following things:

a) Do not remove or fold your tefillin while the congregation is saying *amen, yehei Shemei rabba…* in *Kaddish*, since these words have even more sanctity than the *Kedushah*.[68]

b) Do not remove your *tefillin shel rosh* while you are directly facing an open *Sefer Torah* (since this is considered disrespectful to the *Sefer Torah*) in order not to uncover your head (in front of it). Instead, step back some distance, turn away from the *Sefer Torah,* and then remove your tefillin.[69] On *Rosh Chodesh*, tefillin are removed after the *Kaddish* following *U'va LeTzion* (i.e. just before *Mussaf*), although some people remove their tefillin before that *Kaddish*.[70]

People who have the *minhag* of wearing tefillin on *Chol Hamoed* should remove them before *Hallel*.[71]

May I take off my tefillin in front of my *rebbi*?

You should not remove your *tefillin shel rosh* while standing directly in front of your *rebbi muvhak* (the person who taught you most of your Torah knowledge) in order not to uncover your head in front of him. Instead, turn your body slightly to the side.[72]

RESPECT FOR TEFILLIN

How should I hold the tefillin?

The *bayis* should be held, for it is prohibited to let it hang toward the floor. The *retzuos* may dangle if it is for the purpose of putting on or removing the tefillin, but they should not touch the ground.[73]

If my tefillin are in my bedroom or in my bunk in camp, may I get dressed in front of them?

You may never appear fully undressed in front of uncovered tefillin, *sefarim, siddurim*, or anything with Torah content. Therefore, if there are people who stand naked in the bedroom or the bunk, be sure to keep these items covered with a *non-transparent* covering.[74]

May I sit on a bench that has tefillin on it?

If the tefillin are raised a handbreadth off of the bench (e.g. on a pillow or other object), or if they are resting in a bag, it is permitted.[75] The same applies to *sefarim*.

What should I do if my tefillin fell on the floor?

Nowadays, it is customary to give *tzedakah* and not to fast (as was done in the past), since we are too weak or because fasting will interfere with our Torah learning.[76]

I bought a new tefillin bag. What should I do with my old one?

It must be put into *sheimos* (articles that have some sanctity and are buried) and not thrown into the garbage.[77]

Can I put my *siddur* into my tefillin bag?

The tefillin bag may not be used for anything other than tefillin. However, the plastic bag used to protect the tefillin bag may be used to hold a *siddur* or even a non-mitzvah item.[78]

If I am in the airport and have no place to put my tefillin, may I bring them into the restroom?

As a last resort you may bring your tefillin into a restroom only if the tefillin are in a double covering, i.e. the tefillin bag is placed inside another covering such as a suitcase, or a deep coat pocket, etc. (The plastic tefillin bag and the tallis bag don't count; however, if the tallis covers the tefillin inside the bag, it is acceptable.) The same rule applies if a person is hospitalized and needs to relieve himself while the tefillin are in the room. He may also place the tefillin in the drawer of a cabinet. *Sefarim* (or anything else with Torah content) must also be double-covered in a bathroom; wrapping the *sefer* in a bag and placing it in a pocket will suffice.[79]

May I place tefillin on the ground?

No. However, if there is no other option and the tefillin are resting in a bag, it is permitted.[80]

MISCELLANEOUS *HALACHOS*

If I wear a tallis, should my tefillin bag be kept close to the opening of the tallis bag?

No. Since the tallis is put on before the tefillin, one should not pass over the tefillin bag in order to reach the tallis (*ain ma'avirin al hamitzvos* — you should not pass over mitzvos). Therefore, keep the tallis closest to the opening of the tallis bag.[81]

I came to shul, but I don't have tefillin. What should I do?

You must wear tefillin at least during *Kerias Shema* and *Shemoneh Esrei*.[82] If possible, find a spare kosher pair of tefillin before *davening*. If one is not available, ask somebody if you could borrow his tefillin after he finishes *Shemoneh Esrei*. Until the tefillin become available, *daven* until the end of *Yishtabach* (the prayer before the *berachos* of the *Shema*), wait until the tefillin become available, and then put them on with a *berachah*. Proceed to recite the *berachos* of the *Shema*, *Kerias Shema*, and *Shemoneh Esrei*.[83] However, if the latest time to say *Kerias Shema* will pass in the interim, it is better to finish *davening* without tefillin and later put on tefillin and say *Kerias Shema* or a paragraph of *Tehillim*.[84] You must not let a whole day go by without wearing tefillin.[85]

May I borrow someone else's tefillin without his permission?

You may borrow someone's tefillin without his permission only as long as the following conditions are met:

a) you can't find the owner to ask him.

b) you wrap them up afterwards.

c) you do not remove them from the place in which you found them.

d) you are sure that the owner wouldn't mind if he knew.[86]

Are my tefillin *muktzeh* (a halachic category of items which may not be moved on Shabbos except under special conditions)?

Yes, they are *muktzeh*, and you should therefore remove your *siddur* and tallis from your tefillin bag before Shabbos. If you did not do so, however, you are still allowed to take out your tallis or *siddur* on Shabbos even though you will cause the tefillin to move. Furthermore, you may move them to save them from any kind of damage, or if the place they are occupying is needed for some other purpose.[87]

What rewards are there for the mitzvah of putting on tefillin?

The Torah promises great rewards for putting on tefillin properly:

a) long life.

b) a place in the World to Come.

c) protection from harm from the fires of Gehinnom (Hell).

d) forgiveness for all of one's sins. On the other hand, someone who doesn't put on tefillin because he despises the mitzvah will suffer a severe punishment.[88]

How often should I have my tefillin checked?

Most tefillin today are made from cattle hide, which is thick and durable. Therefore, if they were once checked by a reliable *sofer* they don't have to be checked again. However, if the tefillin became soaked by water, feel a little damp, were exposed to moisture, or have a tear in them, they should be checked immediately. If the tefillin become slightly moist through perspiration, wipe them off after removing them. Tefillin made from thin hide should be checked twice every seven years.[89]

Must I fill in every scratch on my tefillin?

If any scratch is visible on the *retzuah* or on the *bayis,* you should fill it in *immediately*. Most black coloring will do (see endnotes), and you can easily blacken the whitened area yourself. Before doing so, think to yourself, "I'm doing this in order to maintain the sanctity of tefillin."[90]

He who wears tefillin is called king on earth, even as G-d is called King in heaven.

Zohar 3:169b

Tefillin Tidbits

■ If the *tefillin shel rosh* was accidentally put on first, it should be left on and then the *tefillin shel yad* should be put on.[91]

■ When one is unable to put tefillin on either his arm or head, he should nevertheless put on the other. If only the *tefillin shel rosh* is worn, Ashkenazim should say both *berachos*, i.e. *"lehawniach,"* and *"al mitzvas."* If only the *tefillin shel yad* is worn, recite only *" lehawniach."* [92]

■ If you forgot to say the *berachos* on the tefillin, you may say them as long as you are still wearing the tefillin.[93]

■ An equally ambidextrous person puts tefillin on the left arm. When he is ambidextrous but it is not equal, a rabbi should be consulted.[94]

■ A father has an obligation to buy tefillin for his son and to teach him the *halachos* of tefillin.[95]

■ One who loses a parent, wife, or child does not put on tefillin from the time he hears of the death until the second day of *shivah*.[96] (see endnote)

■ One should have peace of mind when he puts on tefillin.[97]

■ One may not touch a dirty diaper while wearing tefillin.[98]

■ One who has had surgery and has a catheter attached to his body may *daven* while wearing tefillin if the bottle is covered.[99]

■ One who is too ill to put on tefillin by himself may have somebody else put them on him, including his son or daughter, even if they are under the age of bar/bas mitzvah, and his wife.[100]

A Deeper Look

Excerpts from

TEFILLIN

by Rabbi Aryeh Kaplan *zt"l*

G-D'S TEFILLIN

Rabbi Avin bar Rav Ada said in the name of Rabbi Yitzchak, "Where do we find that G-d wears tefillin?"

It is written (Isaiah 62:8), "G-d has sworn by His right hand, and by the arm of His strength."

"His right hand" is the Torah, as it is written (Deuteronomy 33:2), "From His right hand came a fiery law for them."

"The arm of His strength" is tefillin, as it is written (Psalms 29:11), "G-d gives strength to His people."

But where do we find that the tefillin are Israel's strength?

It is written (Deuteronomy 28:10), "And the people of the earth shall see that G-d's Name is called upon you, and they shall (see your strength) and be awed by you."

We learned that the great Rabbi Eliezer said, "This is speaking of the tefillin worn on the head."

Rabbi Nachman bar Yitzchak asked Rabbi Chiya bar Avin, "And what is written in the tefillin of the Master of the world?"

He replied that it contains the verse (I Chronicles 17:21), "Who is like Your people Israel, a singular nation on earth, whom G-d went to redeem for Himself for a people, to make Himself a Name, by great and tremendous things."

(Berachos 6a)

We have here one of the most mysterious teachings in the entire Talmud. We are taught that G-d wears tefillin containing the praise of the Jewish people.... We know that G-d is not a material Being, and that He has neither body, shape nor form. We certainly cannot imagine Him wearing tefillin in any physical sense....

But still, our sages were most certainly teaching us an important lesson when they say that G-d wears tefillin. What message does this most remarkable lesson contain?...

Somehow, this lesson appears to teach us about the relationship between G-d and the Jewish people. Our sages teach us that G-d borrows terms from His creatures to express His relationship with the world. But what do these terms represent? We find a hint in Elijah's introduction in the *Tikunei Zohar*, where he says:

> ## Love is the right hand,
> ## Power is the left, Glory is the body,
> ## Victory and splendor are the two feet...
> ## Wisdom is the brain, Understanding is the heart...
> ## And the crown of all is the place where tefillin rest...

G-d created the world with infinite wisdom... but there is something that must come even before wisdom....

What comes even before wisdom?

The answer is purpose, and the will and desire to create.... The crown of all creation is G-d's purpose.

Elijah said, "the crown of all is the place where tefillin rest."

This means that G-d's tefillin are intimately bound to His purpose.... The Talmud asked what are in G-d's tefillin. It answers that it contains the concept of Israel, the Jewish people.

G-d's tefillin are His concept of Israel. When Elijah says, "the crown of all is the place where tefillin rest," he is saying that the concept of Israel is bound to G-d's purpose in creation.

G-d's purpose in creation was to bestow good, and He created the Torah as the means through which man attains this good. Thus, the only ones who can reach the ultimate Good are those who accepted the Torah. The ones who accepted the Torah are the Jewish People.

G-d's original purpose required someone to receive His Good.

In accepting the Torah, Israel became that someone. Thus, the concept of Israel was essentially the first ingredient in creation. This is what our sages mean when they say that the world was created for the sake of Israel....

The main good that G-d offers us is in a transcendental realm beyond this life. It is where man experiences the closeness to G-d, which was His ultimate purpose in creation. This is called *Gan Eden,* Paradise, and the World to Come.

However, for the man who has done evil and remained far from G-d, this is also a time when he must face his Maker. He must experience the burning shame of one who has rebelled against G-d. This burning shame is what we call the fires of Gehinnom.

The Talmud teaches us that a man who is not utterly sinful experiences Gehinnom for a mere moment and is then redeemed. This is alluded to in the passage (I Samuel 2:6), "G-d kills and revives, He brings one down to *She'ol* [the grave], and brings him up again." It is also the meaning of the verse (Zechariah 13:9), "I will bring... them through fire, and refine them like silver, and assay them like gold."

This is only true, however, when a person wears tefillin.... A sinner who wears tefillin may descend to Gehinnom, but he is immediately purified and refined. All the evil he has done can be redeemed and returned to the Holy.

The man who never wears tefillin does not have this means of redemption....

Even if a man sins, as long as he maintains the link of the tefillin, he can still bring himself back to G-d....

Everything in the tefillin is made from an animal product. Man is only perfected through his animal nature, that is, through his physical body. Man's link with G-d is through the physical observance of His commandments.

Everything in tefillin must be made only from kosher animal products. The physical can be raised to the G-dly only when it is not intermingled with evil.

Tefillin begin with four parchments. These must be perfectly white. This alludes to the Infinite Light at the beginning of Creation.

Ultimately, G-d's ways are hidden from man. We can sometimes see what G-d does, but only dimly perceive His purpose. The parchments are therefore hidden in a "black box"....

The head tefillin are inscribed with the letter *shin*. On the right side it is the usual three-headed *shin,* while on the left, it contains four heads. This *shin* is the first letter of G-d's Name, *Sh-dai,* which is spelled out by the letters of the tefillin....

The two straps emanating from the head tefillin to the right and left represent the two basic forces of Creation, love and judgment. While sometimes G-d's love would dictate mercy, His judgment demands retribution. Ultimately, G-d's justice is a combination of the two.

This is represented by the knot, binding the two sides together....

The hand tefillin are bound with a knot in the shape of the letter *yud.* This letter always symbolizes the ultimate good in the World to Come. G-d's action is guided by His ultimate goal which is this future world.

The *yud* is also the final letter of the Name *Sh-dai,* the Name associated with G-d's providence. Together with the *shin* of the head tefillin, and the *dalet* of its knot, the tefillin spell out this Name. The *dalet* in the knot represents G-d's justice in all His actions....

The seven windings on the arm represent...the seven days of Creation.

Adjusting the Head Tefillin Knot*

SQUARE KNOT

Tightening the head tefillin.

Loosening the head tefillin.

DALET KNOT

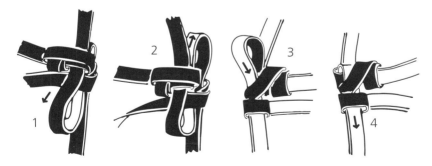

Steps for tightening the head tefillin. Note that only the right-hand strap is made to slide.

To loosen the strap, the exact opposite procedure is followed. The sequence is then 4,3,2,1.

*Illustrations reprinted with permission from N.C.S.Y./Mesorah Publications

True Stories

Jacob, a fifteen-year-old boy from New York, came to a kibbutz in Israel for the summer. He had a terrible accident while working with a certain machine, and his finger was sliced off.

A short while later, Jacob brought his tefillin to a scribe to be checked. The scribe found out that in the phrase *"al yadecha"* — "on your arm," the word *"al"* — "on" — was missing.

One should purchase his tefillin from a G-d-fearing and reliable person, and have them checked if they are exposed to moisture.

Avi was an Israeli tank driver in the war in Lebanon. Of course, he took his tefillin with him wherever he went.

Avi was in the middle of the battle and was driving to a certain destination. Right then, he remembered that he had forgotten his tefillin at the place where the unit had camped the night before. If he wouldn't go back to get them, the tefillin would never be found.

Immediately, Avi turned the tank around in order to retrieve the tefillin. As soon as he turned the tank around and started heading back, a bomb fell on the spot where the tank had been situated just a moment before.

Besides being a special mitzvah, the mitzvah of tefillin watches over us in everything we do.

Bound to His Father

A Story Told by Rabbi Paysach J. Krohn, *shlita**

In the summer of 2000, 16-year-old Mordechai Kaler volunteered to help in the Hebrew Home of Greater Washington in Rockville, Md. One of his responsibilities was to invite the residents to attend the daily services (minyan) in the synagogue on the first floor. Some agreed and others refused, but even those who declined were pleasant about it.

There was one man on the second floor, however, who had been quite nasty and had even cursed another volunteer when he was asked to join the minyan. The volunteer was taken aback by the man's tirade, so Mordechai undertook the challenge of speaking to the angry gentleman.

Mordechai found the man sitting in a wheelchair in a lounge filled with residents of the home. After introducing himself, Mordechai said softly but firmly, "If you don't wish to join the services we can respect that, but why should you curse the volunteer? He is here to help and he was just doing his job."

"Young man," the elderly gentleman said sternly, "wheel me to my room. I want to tell you a story."

When they were in the room alone, the old man told his story of horror, pain and sadness. He came from a prominent religious family in Poland and when he was 12-years-old, he and his family were taken to a Nazi concentration camp. They were all killed except for him and his father.

In their barracks there was a man who had smuggled in the tefillin shel rosh, the leather black box containing biblical passages worn on the head during morning prayers. Every day the men in the barracks

* Reprinted with permission from *Reflections of the Maggid: Inspirational stories from around the globe and around the corner,* by Rabbi Paysach J. Krohn; Artscroll/Mesorah Publications.

would try to seize an opportunity to put on the religious gear, even for a moment, when there were no Nazi S.S. guards nearby. The men knew that they hadn't fulfilled the religious duty because they were missing the second part of the tefillin, for the hand, but their love for doing the Creator's commands compelled them to do whatever they could.

The man continued, "But for my father that wasn't enough. My bar mitzvah was coming up and he wanted that at least on t that day that I wear a complete set of tefillin. He had heard that in a barracks down the road, a man who had been killed had a complete pair of tefillin.

"On the morning of my bar mitzvah, my father, at great risk, went out early to the other barracks to get the tefillin. I was waiting by the window with trepidation. In the distance I could see him rushing to get back. As he came closer I could see that he was carrying something cupped in his hands.

"As he got to the barracks, a Nazi stepped out from behind a tree and shot and killed him right before my eyes! When the Nazi left I ran out and took the pouch of tefillin that lay on the ground next to my father. I managed to hide it."

The old man peered angrily at Mordechai and said vehemently, "How can anyone pray to a G-d Who would kill a boy's father right in front of him? I can't!"

The man pointed to the dresser against the wall and said, "Open the top drawer."

In the drawer Mordechai saw an old black tefillin pouch, crusted from many years of not being used. "Bring me the pouch," the man ordered. Mordechai complied.

The man opened it and took out an old pair of tefillin. "This is what my father was carrying on that fateful day. I keep it to show people what my father died for, these dirty black boxes and straps. These were the last things I got from my father."

Mordechai was stunned. He had no words no comfort to give. He could only pity the poor man who had lived his life in anger, bitterness and sadness. "I'm sorry," he finally stammered softly. "I didn't realize." Mordechai left the room resolved never to come back to the man again. When he came home that evening, he couldn't eat or sleep.

He returned to the home the next day, but avoided the old man's room. A few days later, as Mordechai was helping the men who had come to the synagogue, one of the elderly wanted to recite the prayer said on the anniversary of a death, one that required a quarom.

"I have yahrzeit today and I need to say Kaddish," the elderly man beseeched. "We only have nine men here today. You think you could get a tenth?"

Mordechai had already made his rounds that morning and had been refused by many of the residents. They were too tired, not interested or half asleep. The only one he hadn't approached was the old man on the second floor.

Reluctantly and hesitantly he went upstairs. He knew the old man would scold him, but he still had to make an effort. He knocked on the door gently and announced himself.

"It's you again?" the old man asked.

"I'm so sorry to trouble you," Mordechai said softly, "but there's a man in synagogue who needs to say Kaddish today. We need you for a minyan. Would you mind coming just this one time?"

The old man looked up at Mordechai and said, "If I come this time, then you'll leave me alone?" Mordechai wasn't expecting that response. "Yes," he said in a whisper, "I won't bother you again."

To this day, Mordechai doesn't know why he then said what he did. It could have infuriated the old man, but for some reason Mordechai blurted out, "Would you like to bring your tefillin?"

Mordechai braced himself for a bitter retort – but instead the man said again, "If I bring them, will you leave me alone?" "Yes," Mordechai said, "I will leave you alone."

"All right," the man replied, "then wheel me downstairs and make sure that I'm in the back of the synagogue, so I can get out first."

Mordechai wheeled the old man to the synagogue and brought him to the back. "May I help you?" Mordechai asked as he took the tefillin out of the pouch. The gentleman put out his left hand. Mordechai helped him put on his tefillin and left the synagogue to do other work.

After the services, Mordechai returned and the synagogue was empty – except for the old man. He was still wearing his tefillin and tears were running down his cheeks. "Shall I get a doctor or a nurse?" Mordechai asked.

The man didn't answer. Instead he was staring down at the straps of tefillin wrapped on his left arm, caressing them with his right hand and repeating over and over, "Tatte, Tatte [Father, Father], it feels so right."

The old man then looked up at Mordechai and said, "For the last half hour I've felt so connected to my Tatte. I feel as though he has come back to me."

Mordechai took the man back to his room and as he was about to leave, the old man said, "Please come back for me tomorrow."

And so every morning Mordechai would go to the second floor and the old man would be waiting for him at the elevator holding his tefillin. Mordechai would wheel him into the synagogue where he would sit in the back wearing his tefillin, holding a siddur (prayerbook), absorbed in his thoughts.

One morning Mordechai got off the elevator on the second floor but the man wasn't there. He hurried to his room, but his bed was empty. Instinctively he became afraid. He ran to the nurses' station and asked where the gentleman was – and they told him.

He had been rushed to the hospital the previous afternoon and late in the day he had had a stroke and died.

A few days later, Mordechai was given an award by the Jewish home for his work as a volunteer. After the ceremonies a woman approached him and thanked him for all he had done for her. Mordechai had no recollection of the woman. "Excuse me," Mordechai said, "do I know you?"

"I am the daughter of that man you helped," she said softly. "He was my father and you did so much for him. You made his last days so comfortable. When he was in the hospital he called me frantically and asked me to bring him his tefillin. He wanted to pray one more time with them. I helped him with his tefillin in the hospital and then he had his stroke."

He died wearing them.

Bound to his Father in Heaven.

Heard from Rabbi Zvi Teitelbaum, principal of the Yeshiva of Greater Washington in Silver Spring, Maryland, who I thank for sharing it with me.

Endnotes

A₁   The order of the *parshiyos* in the illustration are according to Rashi. His grandson, Rabbeinu Tam, differs. According to Rabbeinu Tam, the placement of the *Shema* and *Vehayah im shamoa* are in reverse order. The halachah follows the view of Rashi. However, many scrupulous individuals also put on Rabbeinu Tam tefillin.

1   SA 38:2.

2   SA 27:4, MB 14.

3   *Kaf Hachaim* 27 #20; SA 27, MB 16.

4   SA 25:1; if possible, put on your tallis and tefillin in a side room of the synagogue before entering the synagogue proper. See SA 25:2, MB 8.

5   Rabbi Shimon Eider, *Halachos of Tefillin*, p.191.

6   SA 28, MB 7.

7   *Arukh Hashulchan* 40:1.

8   SA 27:2; the black cover may be left on the *tefillin shel yad* when reciting the *berachah*. See *Zichron Eliyahu, siman* 9.

9   SA 28:3; see *Igros Moshe, Orach Chaim* 4:10.

10   SA 25:5, MB 16.

11   SA (Rama) 25:11; *Kaf Hachaim* 25:33.

12   SA 27:1.

13   SA 27:1.

14   SA (Rama) 27:1, MB 4.

15   SA 27, MB 4; in fact, the opinion of the Vilna Gaon is that the upper half of the bicep is also considered the proper place for the placement of the tefillin. Sephardim should consult a *posek* if the tefillin don't fit between the two limits.

16   SA 27, MB 16.

17   SA 25:5; some authorities require you to wash your hands after putting on tefillin if you rubbed your arm above the elbow in the process. There are different opinions on the matter. See *Ben Ish Chai, Parashas Toldos*, #17.

18   SA 25:7.

19   SA 25:8.

20   SA (Rama) 25:11; *Kaf Hachaim* 25:33.

21   SA 27:9-10, MB 33,35.

22   SA 25:5.

23   SA 25:5.

24   SA 25, MB 20.

SA = *Shulchan Arukh*; MB = *Mishnah Berurah*

25 SA (Rama) 25:8; some authorities require you to wash your hands after putting on tefillin, if you rubbed your head in the process. There are different opinions about the matter. See *Tzitz Eliezer* XII, 6:1.

26 SA (Rama) 25:5.

27 SA 27:11, MB 38.

28 SA 28:2, MB 6.

29 SA 25, *Sha'arei Teshuvah*, footnote #15.

30 SA 28, MB 6.

31 SA 28:3.

32 SA 28, MB 9.

33 *Arukh Hashulchan* 28:8.

34 SA 28, MB 9.

35 *Arukh Hashulchan* 28:8.

36 SA 28, MB 6; *Kaf Hachaim* 28:7.

37 SA 28, MB 9; *Halachos of Tefillin,* p. 197.

38 SA 28, MB 7.

39 SA 37, MB 4; See SA (Rama) 656: A person does not have to spend more than a fifth of his money on a mitzvah.

40 SA 32:20; SA 39:8, MB 19.

41 SA 31:1- 2, MB 8: Since there are differing opinions about the necessity of wearing tefillin on *Chol Hamoed*, if you do wear them, do so with the intention of fulfilling the mitzvah only if it applies. (This avoids violation of the prohibition against "*ba'al tosif*" — adding extra mitzvos.)

42 Heard from R' Avigdor Nebenzahl, *shlita,* and R' Yitzchak Berkowitz, *shlita*. There are other customs as well.

43 SA 555:1, MB 5. See R' Shimon Eider's *Halachos of the Three Weeks*.

44 SA 30:1.

45 Heard from R' Berkowitz, *shlita.*

46 SA 30, MB 17.

47 Check the chart in your synagogue/school for the latest time to say *Shema*. It is approximately 3 hours into the day. See SA 58:1, MB 1-9, for explanations of how to calculate the time.

48 SA 38:1-2, MB 7,9; SA 66, MB 40; SA 80:1, MB 1-4.

49 SA 38:1, MB 5.

50 Heard from R' Yakov Friedman, *shlita;* SA 22, MB 3, and *Biur Halachah* "*Kana.*" You may also recite a "*Shehechiyanu*" over a new fruit while wearing your tefillin for the first time.

51 SA 25:5, MB 15.

SA = *Shulchan Arukh*; MB = *Mishnah Berurah*

52   SA 25:9, MB 29.

53   SA 25:10, MB 28,30,32,34,36.

54   SA 25, MB 44.

55   SA 37, MB 3.

56   SA 37, MB 4.

57   SA 61:25, MB 39; SA 28:1, MB 1. Every time one thinks about the tefillin, touch them and check to see that they have not moved out of place.

58   *Ta'amei Haminhagim,* p. 548; SA 59, *Be'er Heitiv,* footnote #1. See SA 25:3, MB 13, regarding *"Otair Yisrael Besifarah."*

59   SA 38, MB 5.

60   *Minchas Yitzchak* 6:13; see *Arukh Hashulchan* 25:23; SA 25, MB 47.

61   SA 38:4.

62   Rambam, *Hilchos Issurei Biah* 22:21.

63   SA 28, *Sha'arei Teshuvah,* footnote #1.

64   SA 40:8, MB 19-20; heard from R' Nebenzahl, *shlita.*

65   SA 44:1; see MB 3-4.

66   SA 79, MB 23; I heard from R' Nebenzahl, *shlita,* that this halachah also applies to tefillin.

67   SA 25:13, MB 55; At the very least, until after *U'va LeTzion.*

68   SA 25:13, MB 56.

69   SA 25:13, MB 58; see *Halachos of Tefillin,* p.148.

70   SA 25:13, MB 59.

71   SA 25:13, MB 60.

72   SA 38:11, MB 36; I heard from R' Yisroel Dzimitrovsky, *shlita,* that nowadays a *rebbi muvhak* is not so common.

73   SA 40:1, MB 2; *Arukh Hashulchan* 40:1.

74   *Arukh Hashulchan* 286:10,14; SA 40, MB 7. As far as the laws of modesty are concerned, you may never stand outside the bathroom (i.e. shower room) fully undressed. Therefore, get dressed under your blanket or in the bathroom (i.e. shower room). See SA 2:1.

75   *Halachos of Tefillin,* p. 160, and heard from R' Nebenzahl, *shlita.*

76   SA 40, MB 3; *Halachos of Tefillin,* p.161; heard from R' Dzimitrovsky, *shlita;* see *Shiurei Berachah* in *Yoreh Deiah* 282:1.

77   SA 42, MB 15.

78   SA 42:3, MB 9,11,16.

79   SA 43, MB 25.

80   SA 43:6, *Biur Halachah "Umainichan."*

81   SA 25, MB 5. If you reach the tefillin bag before reaching the tallis, you are

SA = *Shulchan Arukh*; MB = *Mishnah Berurah*

then required to put the tefillin on first. If you violate this rule and take the tallis out any way, you should put the tallis on first, before the tefillin. According to Minhag Chabad, if one touches the tefillin bag first, one should nevertheless put on the *tallis* before the tefillin. However, if one touches the actual tefillin first, one should put them on before the *tallis*. If the tallis is resting over the tefillin bag, it's advisable to always keep the tallis bag upright so that the tallis does not rest on top of the tefillin.

82 SA 25:4.

83 SA 66, MB 40; *Kaf Hachaim* 53 # 7.

84 SA 25, MB 14; SA 66, MB 40.

85 SA 37, MB 2.

86 SA 25:12, MB 53; SA 14:4, MB 13-15. I heard from R' Yakov Fried, *shlita*, that HaRav Eliyashiv, *shlita*, and HaRav Scheinberg, *shlita*, both maintain that since tefillin are expensive nowadays, you have to be sure the owner would not mind if you would use his tefillin.

87 SA 31:1, MB 2.

88 SA 37:1, MB 1.

89 SA 39:10, MB 26.

90 SA 32, MB 183; SA 33:4. If the paint is made from a non-kosher animal, it is forbidden to use on the tefillin. Tefillin touch-up paint with a reliable certification (*hekhsher)* may be found at most Jewish book stores. I heard from R' Nebenzahl, *shlita,* that one should be stringent to also fill in a scratch on the *bayis.*

91 SA 25:6, MB 22.

92 SA 26:1-2, MB 3.

93 SA 26:2, MB 3; SA 25, MB 32: Move the *bayis* out of place on the arm, make the *berachah,* and move it back into place. Do the same for the *tefillin shel rosh.*

94 SA 27:6.

95 SA 37:3, MB 9; see the *Bach* and *Eliya Rabbah, siman* 17.

96 SA 38:5, MB 16; speak to a knowledgeable rabbi about this law and all other laws that pertain to a mourner.

97 SA 38:9, MB 31.

98 SA 43:9; *Halachos of Tefillin*, p. 142.

99 *Igros Moshe, Orach Chaim* 1:27.

100 I heard from R' Dovid Morgenstern, *shlita*, that the mitzvah is to wear tefillin; therefore, even one who is not obligated to wear tefillin may put tefillin on one who is ill. See SA 27, MB 6.

SA = *Shulchan Arukh*; MB = *Mishnah Berurah*

Glossary

Ashkenazim – Jews of European ancestry.

bar mitzvah – a Jewish boy who at 13 years of age assumes religious responsibilities.

bas mitzvah – a Jewish girl who at 12 years of age assumes religious responsibilities.

bayis (batim) – the black casings that house the *parshiyos.*

berachah (berachos) – a blessing.

Chol Hamoed – the middle days of the Pesach and Succos holidays.

daven – pray.

Halachah (halachos) – Jewish law.

Hashem – G-d.

Kerias Shema – see *Shema.*

kosher – acceptable according to Jewish law.

ma'abarta – the portion of the base of the tefillin through which the black strap passes.

Mashiach – Messiah.

Minchah – the afternoon prayer service.

minhag (minhagim) – custom or tradition.

mitzvah (mitzvos) – a commandment.

Mussaf – the additional prayer service on Shabbos, *Rosh Chodesh*, and holidays.

parashah (parshiyos) – a Torah portion.

retzuah (retzuos) – the black leather strap.

Rosh Chodesh – the first day of the Jewish month.

sefer (sefarim) – a book of religious content.

Sefer Torah – a Torah Scroll.

Sephardim – Jews of Spanish or Oriental ancestry.

Shacharis – the morning prayer service.

Shehechiyanu – the blessing recited over a new and special garment or a new fruit.

Shema – the prayer recited daily proclaiming the Oneness of G-d and affirming faith in Him and His Torah.

Shemoneh Esrei – the central prayer which is recited three times daily.

shivah – the seven-day mourning period following a death.

shlita – an acronym which means "may he live a good and long life."

shul – synagogue.

siddur (siddurim) – prayer book.

sofer – a Jewish scribe.

tallis – a prayer shawl.

tefillin shel rosh – the tefillin worn on the head.

tefillin shel yad – the tefillin worn on the arm.

Tehillim – Psalms.

Tishah b'Av – the ninth day of the Jewish month of Av, the most historically tragic day of the year.

titurah – a square base on which the *bayis* rests.

Torah – the body of Divine knowledge and law found in the Jewish Scriptures and tradition.

tzedakah – charity.

yarmulke – skullcap.

zt"l – an acronym which means "may the righteous person be of blessed memory."

Recommended Books

Halachos of Tefillin, by Rabbi Shimon Eider, Feldheim Publishers

Tefillin: an illustrated guide, by Mosheh Chanina Neiman, Feldheim Publishers

Tefillin, by Rabbi Aryeh Kaplan, NCSY/Mesorah Publications

Tefillin, by Rabbi Moshe Shlomo Emanuel, Targum Press, Feldheim Publishers

Dedicated in Loving Memory of

Samuel Ehrman

שמואל פנחס בן יעקב צבי ע״ה

כ״ד ניסן תשל״ב

Anna Ehrman

חנה בת יצחק יונה ע״ה

ר״ח סיון תשכ״ד

Ralph Loebenberg

רפאל בן מרדכי ע״ה

י״ג אלול תשס״ו

by Fred and Suzan Ehrman

This Sefer is Dedicated By
Michele and Dovid Spira
in Loving Memory
of our Grandparents:

Sarah and Jack Fuchs ז"ל
Molly and Bernhard Spira ז"ל
Charles Krengel ז"ל
Izzy Goldberg ז"ל

May the mitzvah of tefillin
be enhanced to the readers
through this most worthy sefer

Alyssa Ehrman and Mar
Loebenberg
and family

לזכר נשמת
שלום משה בן אברהם ז"ל
our dear friend and role model.

May the mitzvos upon which
Michael centered his life,
be the focal point of those
who have learned from him
and who will continue to grow
because they had the זכות
of knowing and loving him.
May Michael's memory
be an inspiration to all.

נפטר ביום ג' שבט תש"ס

Dedicated by friends of Michael Selesny

לזכר נשמת
משה בן ירמיהו הלוי ז"ל
(Nicholas Goldner)

by his niece and nephew
Debbie and Elliot Gibber

לזכרון עולם בהיכל ה'
ר' יעקב יוסף
בן ר' שלמה
בערנשטיין ז"ל

נפטר ביום כ"ד מרחשון תשנ"ח

לזכרון עולם בהיכל ה'
מוהר"ר גבריאל אליהו
בן הרב נפתלי יוסף הלוי
קלצקו ז"ל

נפטר ביום י"ט מרחשון תשנ"ט